Memories

From the

Rain

AF486068

by

Michael D. McCracken

Memories from the Rain

Copyright © 1993, 2020 by Michael D. McCracken

All rights reserved under International and Pan-American copyright conventions.

ISBN: 9798589146103

Dedication

This book is dedicated to Mrs. Jeanette Deem.

A high school English teacher who had

confidence in my abilities. Merci!

Table of Contents
Part I – Thoughts

<u>Part II – Dreams</u>

<u>Part III – Memories</u>

<u>ACKNOWLEDGEMENTS</u>

"Psychedelic Used Car Lot Blues", by Southbound Freeway, © 1967 Tera Shirma Music.

"Time", by Alice Cary, ©1865, and ©1882 by Houghton, Mifflin and Company

A Wisp of Smoke

A wisp of smoke
dancing lightly in the setting sun.
First here, then there,
moving in all directions at once.

Spirits move you,
playing their thousand little games.
Or are you not
floating freely across the plains?

Little wisp of smoke
drifting slowly to the clouds,
did you really know
that there won't be any crowds?

Floating aimlessly -
you have nowhere to go.
Part yourself, once, twice;
who is going to know?

Inward and out,
up, down , and around,
float with the wind,
for you can't be bound.

A wisp of smoke
how well it spreads!
No longer here,
for now it's dead.

My Watch

Just now I picked up my watch
to put it on again.
It had lain on the dresser
for a few days.
I remember putting it there
so I'd be free of its demands
if just for a little while.
But the taste of freedom -
being away from it -
was too delicious
so that only now
am I willing
to return it to my wrist.
I looked at it -
the very tick-tock
of its inner soul was silent -
and it made me pause to think
maybe too profound a thought:
No matter how important
we think ourselves to be,
Time doesn't stop,
not even for death.

Thinking

Sometimes I think about life.
Sometimes I think about death.
Sometimes I think about the number 3.

People come up to me and mess up my mind,
People talk to me, but I don't understand.
People everywhere, but are the really there?

Many times I think about a lot of things,
But not today; it's my day off,

A Leaf

A leaf is a fragile thing,
yet frailness is one with strength.

A leaf is a plain thing,
yet plainness is also beauty.

A leaf is rough,
yet roughness hides tenderness.

A leaf is much like love,
for without love, there is nothing

A Woman

A woman is a special person.
She can be soft,
fragile and sweet -
or furious and raging
like wounded cheetah.

A woman makes herself pretty.
Sometimes to please her man,
other times to please herself,
or just for no reason at all.

A woman can be understanding,
fair and gentle,
or the "Green Monster"
can turn her into a cruel,
harsh and evil being.

A woman has many faults;
Man has many more,
but even with all their little
quirks and fancies,
a Woman is a very special person.

The Note

Today I received a little note,
which I wish the Dean had never wrote.
It said my request for eighteen hours
would cost me another two thousand dollars.
And all because of this bald jester
I've to attend one more semester.
I would like to thank him very much
for having such a humane touch.
And if the chance does come to pass,
I'd like him ousted on his ...

Nothing

Mindless wanderings
through endless mazes
the threshold of eternity
hears destiny call

The Root Of All Evil

Money,
Money is the root of all evil.
It can cause greed,
avarice, and hatred
even between brothers.

It causes men to become
miserly, and foolish;
and women to be
vain and selfish.

Not enough money causes
death and poverty;
while too much causes
arrogance and brutality.

The more money one has,
the more one....

You'll have to excuse me now;
I have to go.
I have to make some more money
so I can afford to write
more poetry.

A Melancholy Song

There was a time, when I was young
that laughter filled the air.
The life I led, the songs I'd sung
were done without a care.

I had no goals, and had no dreams,
I had no sense at all.
My life was wrought with thought and screams;
that led to my downfall.

Though much was lost, in those sad years
time has not passed me by.
I saw my faults, and gripped my fears;
now see life eye to eye.

A Special Thing

One thing I'll give you -
it's precious to me.
You must return it
for then you'll see
I still have my own
while yours has been freed.
If you pass it along
then the smile will be
a very special thing.

Life In 1984
(A future look on a past occurrence)

Have your ever wondered
what it would be like,
to live in 1984?

To have your lives monitored
like an insect under the microscope?
To become a number,
so that everything you do
can be traced to your number?

Or how would you like
to pick your child from a test tube,
without blemish or flaws?
Why care if you're sterile
or impotent,
there's enough test tubes
for everyone.

How would you like
to see a phone call?
or live in outer space
for a year?
Maybe even fly
with your own air car?

Have you ever wondered
what it would be like?
Take a good look around you,
because it's reality.

In The Midst Of Plenty

In this world of plenty,
there are shortages;
shortages of beef,
of grain, and also paper.

We are low on fuels,
and clean air and water;
the list gets longer
everyday we live.

So many things are
we short of,
it makes a person wish -
wouldn't it be nice
if we had a shortage
of shortages?

Love Is ...What?

Love, what is it?
What power does this word possess
that makes it strike down the strongest man,
and causes women to swoon and go light in the head?

What spell 'tis cast by saying
"I Love You"?
Does this bind the two together,
or is it said just for the moment?
A moment when only tenderness matters.

Love! Love 'tis a falsehood.
The more it's said,
the less it' meant.

Affection, whether it be tempered with
genuine warmth and respect,
is a far better measure of feeling
than love.

Here At The Bus Station

A girl with a baby;
a couple of old ladies;
a few men wandering around;
it was depressing
watching these people
here at the bus station.

It seemed like everyone was afraid;
afraid of being mugged;
or raped or maybe killed;
but nobody talked
to anybody else
here at the bus station.

No one tried to converse;
or crack a joke or two;
or try to become friends
with anyone else;
too afraid of losing their dignity
here at the bus station.

Goin' Down 75

Goin' down 75,
what a lonely stretch of road.

Snaking through the big city;
crawling through the farmlands
takes forever to travel.

Or so it seems anyway,
maybe it's just my imagination;
maybe not.
But goin' down 75
just ruins my whole day.

What Goes Up Must Come Down

You've heard the old saying
"What goes up must come down",
and how cold air
stays close to the ground
while hot air rises
to the clouds.
It makes me wonder
how politicians keep on the ground.

This Monotonous Life

Do you ever get tired,
I mean really tired?
Tired of little things
and big things;
of the everyday
and not so common things?

Tired of being alone,
yet always being with someone;
tired of talking to people
who don't understand
what you've just said?

Or really working hard
and never getting anything finished?
Tired of just suffering each day
only to start again the next day -
the minute you wake up?

You know it's depressing,
but you'll get over it,
you always do.
Then you'll become
another blank body -
one of the crowd.

People

They tell us not to get involved.
But what do they know?
Could it be they are jealous,
or maybe old and calloused?
I listen not to such absurdities.
For I know the truth -
to get involved is what we live for,
nothing less, nothing more.

Death Personified

Death -
the immortal unfeeling spectre,
of which Man cannot fight.
With his book of names he stalks;
patiently, as a feline on the hunt,
waiting for the right moment to strike.

He knows none can escape him,
so uncaringly he chooses his next victim.
Man, infant, woman, child,
it makes no difference,
they will all die by his hand.

Death -
the sinister being;
be he Grim Reaper, Fate, or Norn,
Man's fear of him is boundless.
To what would it avail him fight?
Nothing, nothing at all.

The land is filled
with the lust of Death.
To him it is a game
to take one's life away,
while we have no armour,
no lance to fight with.

Who knows when next Death strikes?
Only he knows, only he.

Stallions In The Night

Dust clouds on the plains
The whinny of wild horses
Hooves pounding the dirt

Wonder In The Grass

I settled among the grass blades,
to rest in the warm sunshine.
I soon reached a sleepy state,
brought on by the gentle wind
brushing against my face.

I seemed alone,
alone with myself,
but that was only for a little while,
because no one's ever completely alone.

A small animal crawled its way up
a tall weed near where I sat,
and I became aware of it
when it landed on my knee.

Its color was bright purple
and it moved very fast
with its many legs
churning away beneath it.

While I marveled at this small wonder
it stopped,
and looked at me,
and it was almost like it knew
I couldn't become a friend,
and it flew away in the next few moments.

Above The Clouds

We drifted along
high above the clouds;
floating, it seemed,
without purpose.

The stars seemed much closer to us
as we talked but said nothing.
My love and I were lost;
as one, among strangers.

Below us we could see
small lights,
coming from some unrecognizable town.

She softly sighed,
put her head on my shoulder,
and we both drifted off
into a dreamlike sleep.

Karen The Magnificent

*They say good things come
in small packages,
Ah, then this little package
must be super.*

*Her eyes flash with a quick
and bright pleasantness,
and her wit is keen,
but good-natured.*

*No man could want another,
once Karen has walked by;
the gods themselves
are at a loss for words
when they try to describe
Karen's natural beauty
and charm.*

*What more can I say about
this dynamic little package?
Quoth the raven
"Nothing more!"*

A Startling Realization

*The snow crunched beneath our feet
as we made our way up the driveway;
the sun had just begun its daytime journey
and the clouds were turning a rosy scarlet.*

*We sat at the table
and watched the snowflakes
as they drifted slowly to the ground.*

*We talked but said nothing
and I looked into her eyes,
and she smiled.*

*For a moment I was flustered,
and words escaped me;
for I suddenly realized
that I had fallen in love with her.*

The Senses of Love

*A touch of love
a taste of sweetness
dwell within two bodies tonight.*

*Your eyes tell all;
but does heart listen?
Your heart has a mind of its own.*

*Friendship and trust
are the bonds of love;
truth and security, the seal.*

*Our love will last
with eyes to guide us;
with heart to listen
and our wisdom enduring
forever.*

Night Time

Night time, quiet time -
a time when the mind's free to roam.
Free to wander at will
with time being lost in your journey.

Night time, peaceful time -
go where your soul longs to go.
For your soul has no bounds
and only restricted by memory.

Night time, wondrous time -
so much to see, feel and hear.
But time is far too short
and even now it's time to return.

Night time, quiet time...

Unforgettable

We sat by the waterfall
watching the water cascade
into the bubbly pool
in front of us.

We talked about ourselves,
our futures, and everything
else we could think of.

By the edge of the pool,
under some tall, cool shade trees
we made love
with the spray from the falls
sprinkling our bodies
with a soft mist

We swam for hours it seemed,
in the secluded cove,
and enjoyed the pleasure
of being with each other.

It was a day I shall remember
and cherish for all time.

Feelings Of Autumn

Driving home on a wet and dreary day,
I was struck by the fact;
it's autumn!

For while I passed all the scarlets,
oranges and greens of the forest
it was obvious,
truly it was autumn!
For no other time are the trees
revealed in their full splendor.

The many fields I drive by;
now all barren and deserted
after harvest time,
matched my own depressed mood.

Even though autumn is a colorful
and beautiful period of time,
it still foreshadow the period -
called winter -
when it seems like everything dies.

This fact didn't help my depression
at all, so I decided
I didn't like autumn
and thought about moving to Florida

A Heavenly Glance

A clear blue sky,
whitewater rolling in on the beach,
sea gulls resting on the sand.

A heavenly glance -
a wondrous feeling.

A Lazy Day

I remember the day well;
floating down the river
singing lazy songs
and not caring about anything.

It was very peaceful
watching the fish
as they darted about
beneath the water.

We watched the clouds
as they drifted above us,
and wished the ride would never end.

We were in love,
not just with each other,
but with the time
we were in.

Girls in Bars

One thing I've noticed
hanging out in bars;
the girls that show the most
are the "won't go fars".

The many girls around here
sure show a lot of skin.
But though you try your best
their pants you won't get in.

Although you're in despair
there still may be a chance
some girl will pick you up,
right after the next dance.

Last Night

Rock music blasted my ears,
lights flashed in myriads of patterns;
it made my head swim last night.

People danced to the beat,
bobbing to and fro;
the music pounded through my head
and made me feel like I was drunk.

Flash, flash went the lights -
beat, beat went the music.
This place makes me forget my troubles;
I can't think about anything here,
not even about the one I love.

There's this woman in black
dancing near me,
why don't I try to pick her up?
(I'd give anything
to be by her side this night).

But as always happens,
my head will clear
in the morning,
and I'll forget what I saw
last night.

Sunday Morning: The Aftermath

Pulsating veins,
illusions of grandeur:
She looked beautiful in the bar -
with the haze of smoke
and the reek of beer -
only to wake up in the morning
to find streaked lipstick,
runny rouge,
and a fat bod next to me.

Why Is Life Not Like A Game?

Life is so fruitless at times.
People expect too much from a person -
nothing ever seems worthwhile anymore.

They expect a person to be somber
and serious all the time;
when life is more than just that:
Life is enjoying people,
Life is trying to get a little smile
on someone's face
even if you have to play the fool.

Life is not caring about the future,
but living every day
as though you'd
never see another.

(cont'd)

(cont'd)

*Life means doing the things you like
rather than becoming a robot
and doing one thing over and over.*

*Life means being able to choose
whether to go out
or stay home and watch T.V.*

*Life means -
well what does it mean?
It would be much simpler
if life were a game
you could start and stop
when things didn't go right,
and start again
when you felt like it.*

*Yes, wouldn't it be easier
if life were a game?
It isn't
but I'll continue to play along.*

Walking In The Snow

I went walking last night
out and about in the snow.
It was so peaceful and quiet
with no one around.

The snow crunched beneath my feet,
and my breath froze my mustache
and tingled my very soul.

There wasn't a car to be found,
and as I walked
I hummed a few songs to myself
and noticed the waves of whiteness
that surrounded me.

(cont'd)

(cont'd)

*I could hear the stoplights blinking
as I passed underneath them,
and was astonished
by the brightness of their light.*

*As I approached home,
I noticed the snow
had been pushed into big
piles along the sidewalk,
and it made for
interesting musing.*

*Moving up the stairs
I glanced out the window -
it was snowing again.
And I sat there dreaming
about the snowflakes
as they came down;
it was a peaceful feeling.*

Riding One Day

An early morning ride
on such a sunny day;
We'll travel untouched paths,
just point to guide our way.

The gentle brushing breeze
caress our every move.
Two people ride together;
two people sharing love.

The far-off distant trees
get larger every mile.
Such sights and smells and sounds
brings to us both a smile.

Two hearts now heading home
against the setting sun.
Two riders are together,
two hearts are now but one.

Dorothy

She sits demurely
upon the couch
her eyes now staring
into the unreachable darkness
that lies within her mind.

She rises now;
her lithe, young form
moves toward me,
a smile on her sensuous lips.

Her hair is soft
and glows in the shimmering twilight;
her voice is like the freshness
of a spring day.

Beautiful, yet graceful;
these are the qualities
that make up the woman
named Dorothy.

Unrequited Love

Is it the night
or the long awaited day
that make the wait
an unbearable masquerade?

It seems as time marches
in its unceasing parade,
and my soul's tears fall
in an endless cascade.

Then my heart reaches out
if just to be saved;
for only your touch
can make me be stayed.

Time

by Alice Cary

What is time, O glorious Giver,
With its restlessness and might,
But a lost and wandering river
Working back into the light?

Every gloomy rock that troubles
Its smooth passage, strikes to life
Beautiful and joyous bubbles
That are only born through strife.

Overhung with mist-like shadows,
Stretch its shores away, away,
To the long, delightful meadows
Shining with immortal May:

Where its moaning reaches never,
Passion, pain, or fear to move,
And the changes bring us ever
Sabbaths and new moons of love.

Joseph Moore

I'll tell you 'bout a friend of mine -
he's really quite a guy.
His story is quite int'resting -
I'm sure you will see why.

His name was Joseph;
Joseph Moore.
He's only ten years old.
T'was loved throughout the neighborhood,
or so from what I'm told.

He'd walk the streets so late at night,
his smile both big and wide.
His younger friends would follow him
and try to match his stride.

His name was Joseph; Joseph Moore.
He's only ten years old.
But if you had a friend like him,
he'd be as good as gold.

(cont'd)

(cont'd)

His friends called him Tarzan of the street,
they also called him Bond.
Sometimes he felt like Sherlock Holmes
'til early hours of dawn.

His name was Joseph; Joseph Moore.
He's only ten years old.
You never knew just what he did
because he never told.

And then one day, not long ago,
he came to his demise -
A speeding car, a drunken man, -
you should have heard the cries!

His name was Joseph; Joseph Moore.
'Twas only ten years old.
Was loved throughout the neighborhood;
and now his story's told.

A Stranger

A woman
dressed -in blue;
she moves like a cat -
so graceful yet refined.

Her name I don't know -
I probably never will -
yet she is something special
if she could only know.

I'd like to get her all alone
but I'll never get the chance
to tell her just how much
a woman she is to me.

So, I must resign myself
to dreams, whims and hopes.
There'll never be any like her
and a stranger
she'll remain.

To Carol

She sits quietly
in the chair across from me.
Her golden-brown hair
glistening in the soft light.

Her eyes shine with an inner strength
and though she seems shy,
her smile bespeaks her friendliness.

Her womanhood is evident,
as she moves about the room.
Hers is one shape that's
not easy to forget.

All in all,
the woman called Carol,
is truly a wondrous sight.

A Broken Heart

*Her heart
broken with thoughts
of yesterdays,
caused her sorrow to go deep.*

*She knew only the love
for another
would sustain her grief.*

*Before,
she was gay and alive;
now, she was listless
and sullen.*

*Through him
she knew love;
now she knows nothing but sorrow.*

*She wished she could tell
how he felt -
whether he felt
the pain of loneliness too.*

*She lowered he head;
she closed her eyes,
and wept.*

My Girl

I can still see her in my mind;
shoulder-length blonde hair,
dazzling jade-green eyes,
and a figure that dares to cry
"Perfection".

She is very much a woman,
yet she knows how to please her man
in so many little ways.

Personality, charm,
poise, and agility
are all qualities
this woman possesses.

This woman is special to me,
as if you couldn't tell,
and should you not know her,
well, I'll tell you -
she's my girl.

The Will Of Body And Mind

Did the Lord send her from his heavenly domain?
For she is so fresh and spirited in mind.
Her form is so refined with femininity
that every step she takes
leaves the imprint of a woman.

Did it happen by chance, or was it His will?
When his eyes beheld her,
the voice of love entered his heart.

As she approached,
she touched his waiting face gently,
and with careful intentions
their lips meet.

His words of closeness filled every corner
of her mind,
and the mind began to wander with will.

His explorations were sincere and soothing
to the one he loved.
And she , in turn, acknowledged his movements.

They were as one,
in perfect harmony.
And they knew
the will of the body
had been dealt with wisdom.

Psychedelic Used Car Lot Blues
by Southbound Freeway

As I was walking down Livernois Street,
on a Friday afternoon,
Strange lookin' cat up and grabbed me by the arm.
I said, "Unhand me, gray-beard loon!"

He had paisley pants and a bear-skin vest,
and a smile all around his face.
I knew right away he had something to sell,
and this is what he says.

"Come with me, and you will see
things you'd never'd thought.
At Freak-Out Freddies, Op-Art Arnold's
Psychedelic Used Car Lot."

"Now here's a set of wheels for a dollar down,
and a dollar a week to pay.
It was owned by a famous rock-and-roll star,
who only drove it to the bank each day."

"It's got paisley seats and stroboscopic lines,
and an incense-burning exhaust,
and dual crystal mirrors that'd blow your mind,
and a map in case you get lost."

(cont'd)

(cont'd)

"Other groovies you will dig,
and these can only be bought,
At Freak-Out Freddies, Op-Art Arnold's
Psychedelic Used Car Lot."

"Now I'm sorry if you found that all the wheels are round,
but there are other things to keep you occupied.
Like a psychedelic version of a Shirley Temple flick,
and you can use the fancy dashboard as you ride."

"And there are iridescent colors in the finger-painted vintage
with organic strewels growing from the floor.
And a psychedelic dash in case of psychedelic trash,
and it takes you out the psychedelic door."

I screamed I had enough of all this psychedelic stuff,
and I ran out seeing psychedelic spots.
From Freak-Out Freddies, Op-Art Arnold's
Psychedelic Used Car Lot.

To Phyllis

I thought of you again today -
you're in someone else's eyes now -
you're never far away from my mind.

I see you everywhere -
I've seen your head
turn in a crowd,
and see your hand
reach for another -
and sometimes I think I see
your silhouette glide by
in the darkness of my dreams.

Forgive me, I love you still!
Can you remember me,
or shall pleasant memories
be forever forgotten?

Memories From The Rain

Raindrops
falling to the ground
remind me of other times,
some of which I had forgotten, until now.

We use to run through the field,
laughing and dancing as we
darted among the raindrops,
getting wonderfully soaked, together.

Acting like scarecrows,
we let the rain touch our faces
and run down our bodies,
while we laughed at each other's funny poses.

The wetness of the grass
had a sensual, exciting quality to it.
We walked together
not saying anything,
but feeling everything.

Raindrops
falling to the ground
remind me of other times...
But that was so very long ago -
I wish I could have them back again.

I Wish You Wouldn't Go

The leaves are falling now -
I hate to see them go.
Seems like only yesterday
I waited patiently for them
to blossom and grow.

During the long, warm summer
we grew to know each and
understand each other.
But summer never lasts forever,
and neither can a summer love.

All around the leaves are falling.
Wish they'd stay a little longer;
wish you'd stay a little longer.

My Family

My family is a house of time.
I've seen it grow, I've seen it shine.
I've seen my children laugh and play,
and watched them grow up through each day.
But now they've grown and gone away,
and I sit and ponder yesterday.

Love once abounded between these walls
and many's the night I still recall.
But those, too, are gone my friend
as my days come to an end.
Yet when I'm dead and laid to rest,
my family's been the very best.

www.ingramcontent.com/pod-product-compliance
Lightning Source LLC
Chambersburg PA
CBHW081359160726
48000CB00010B/3411